The
Stations
of the
Cross

By REV. LAWRENCE G. LOVASIK, S.V.D.
Divine Word Missionary

NIHIL OBSTAT: James T. O'Connor, S.T.D., *Censor Librorum*
IMPRIMATUR: ✝ James P. Mahoney, D.D., *Vicar General,*
Archdiocese of New York
© 1981 *by Catholic Book Publishing Corp., NJ*— Printed in China

ISBN 978-0-89942-299-2

CPSIA   November 2019   10 9 8 7 6 5 4 3   L/P

Introduction

J ESUS Christ, the Son of God, lived, suffered, and died for us. Then He rose again in triumph over sin and death.

At the Last Supper, Jesus gave us Holy Mass as a living remembrance of His Death and Resurrection. The Mass is the same sacrifice that He offered to the Father on the Cross.

We can also remember Jesus's suffering and death by making the Stations of the Cross at any time, especially on Fridays and during all the days of Lent.

The beautiful pictures in this book will help us see how much Jesus suffered for love of us. The simple words will help us tell Jesus of our love and gratitude.

Indulgences — Those who devoutly make the Stations of the Cross may gain a plenary indulgence, which can be applied to the Poor Souls in Purgatory.

PRAYER
BEFORE SAYING
THE STATIONS of the CROSS

JESUS, I want to make
this way of the Cross
to show how much I love You
and thank You,
and to tell You how sorry I am
for having hurt You by my sins.

I wish to gain all the indulgences I can
and offer them for the Poor Souls
in Purgatory,
especially for our family and friends.

Mary, Mother of Sorrows,
be with me,
and help me to pray well.

1st STATION

PILATE CONDEMNS JESUS

JESUS, the people want You to die.
They tell lies about You,
but You do not say a word.

Then the soldiers beat You with whips
and put a crown of thorns on Your
head.
They laugh at You and hit You,
and then they condemn You to death.

You suffer all this quietly
because I disobeyed God's Law.

When You judge my soul after I die,
be kind to me and forgive me!

Lord Jesus crucified,
have mercy on me!

6

2nd STATION

JESUS TAKES HIS CROSS

JESUS, You take up the Cross
which my sins made for You.
You are ready to die for me.

Teach me to carry my cross each day
for love of You,
as you carried Your Cross
for love of me.

When I must suffer let me say,
"Your will be done!"
Help me to save my soul,
which was so dear to You.

Lord Jesus crucified,
have mercy on me!

JESUS FALLS TO THE GROUND FOR THE FIRST TIME

JESUS, by Your first fall
under the heavy Cross,
make up for my pride
which led me into sin.

Make me humble and kind
that I may be like You.

When I fall into some sin,
help me to get up again
by being sorry for the sin
and by trying very hard
never to hurt You again.

Lord Jesus crucified,
have mercy on me!

4th STATION

JESUS MEETS HIS MOTHER

JESUS, You meet Your dear Mother Mary
    who is very sad
    because she sees how much You
      suffer,
    and You never did any wrong.

Her pain is very great
    because she loves You so much.

O my Mother Mary, I am sorry
    for having hurt Jesus and you.

Make me love Jesus as you did
    and help me to be good
    that I may save my soul.

Lord Jesus crucified,
    have mercy on me!

5th STATION

SIMON HELPS JESUS CARRY HIS CROSS

JESUS, the men make Simon help You
to carry Your heavy Cross,
because You are very tired.

I want to help You carry the Cross
by saying, "Jesus, all for You"
when I have something hard to bear.

You told me to carry my Cross
that I may be like You.

I want to walk after You each day
with my cross on my shoulder
to show how much I love You.

Lord Jesus crucified,
have mercy on me!

14

6th STATION

VERONICA WIPES THE FACE OF JESUS

JESUS, Veronica has pity on You
and gives You a cloth
on which You leave the picture
of Your holy face.

Put Your picture on my heart
that I may always think of You
and thank You for all You did
to save my sinful soul.

Make me kind and pure
that You may always see in my soul
a picture of Yourself.

Lord Jesus crucified,
have mercy on me!

7th STATION

JESUS FALLS TO THE GROUND FOR THE SECOND TIME

JESUS, my sins made You fall once again
under Your heavy Cross.

I hope to get Your grace
by going to Confession
and Holy Communion often
and by saying my prayers
to keep me from falling into sin.

Give me light to see what to do
and strength to do it.

All my life let me never stop trying
to do Your holy Will.

Lord Jesus crucified,
have mercy on me!

JESUS MEETS THE WOMEN OF JERUSALEM

JESUS, the good women are crying
to see You in such pain.

You tell them not to cry
but to be sorry for their sins
and the sins of their children.

Help me to be very sorry
for having offended You
when I disobeyed my heavenly
Father.

Please forgive me, Jesus,
and never let me hurt You
by any willful sin.

Lord Jesus crucified,
have mercy on me!

9th STATION

JESUS FALLS FOR THE THIRD TIME

JESUS, You take each step to Calvary
for love of me, to save my soul.
You fall again,
and yet You try to reach the top
where You will die.

How little I try to do the things
that give You joy.

I find it hard to obey,
even to think of You and pray,
and offer up some little pain
to show You how much I love You
and that I really care.

Lord Jesus crucified,
have mercy on me!

THE SOLDIERS TEAR OFF
JESUS' CLOTHES

JESUS, at last You come to Calvary.
Like a lamb led to death
You do not say a word, but pray.

You are ready to give Your life for me.

The soldiers tear off Your clothes,
and Your wounds begin to bleed
again.

Take away from me anything at all
that may keep me from loving You.

Make my heart pure and kind
and fill it with Your grace;
then offer me to God with You.

Lord Jesus crucified,
have mercy on me!

11th STATION

JESUS IS NAILED TO THE CROSS

JESUS, how it must have hurt
    when the men hammered large nails
    into Your hands and feet
    and lifted up the Cross.

Let me never forget that
    when I commit a mortal sin
    it is like nailing You again,
    because You died to take away my
        sins.

Let me see how wicked sin is
    and how good You are.

For three hours You hang
    and bleed for me.

Lord Jesus crucified,
    have mercy on me!

12th STATION

JESUS DIES ON THE CROSS

JESUS, dying on the Cross,
　　I thank You for Your sacrifice
　　which took away my sins
　　and gave me grace to be God's friend
　　and to live as His good child.

I thank You for Your love and mercy
　　and for all the pain You felt
　　to win my soul from the devil
　　and to lead me to heaven someday.

As You died for love of me,
　　may I live and die for You.

Lord Jesus crucified,
　　have mercy on me!

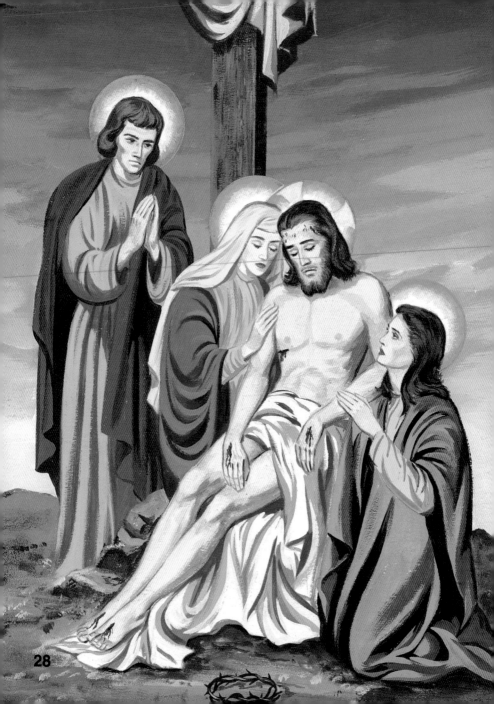

13th STATION

JESUS IS TAKEN FROM THE CROSS

JESUS, Your friends put Your body
    into Your Mother's arms.

Thirty-three years before,
    she gave You to us,
    a sweet Child of Bethlehem.
    Now we give You back to her
    torn, bleeding, and dead.

Our sins have cut her heart
    like a sharp sword of sorrow,
    yet she prays for us, her children,
    for You gave her to us as a mother
    when You were dying on the Cross.

Lord Jesus crucified,
    have mercy on me!

14th STATION

JESUS IS LAID IN THE TOMB

JESUS, Your Mother's heart was broken
   when she saw Your dead body
   lying in the tomb.

She gave You up to die for me —
   how much she must have loved me!

For her sake please forgive me
   and help me to save my soul
   for which You suffered and died.

Mother of Sorrows, pray for me,
   now and at the hour of my death.

Lord Jesus crucified,
   have mercy on me!

PRAYER AFTER THE STATIONS

JESUS, I believe that after three days
    You rose from the dead on Easter
      Sunday,
    and You conquered the devil and
      death.

I thank You for saving my soul,
    and I hope that I, too,
    will rise again in glory
    after the Last Judgment,
    so that with body and soul
    I may praise You forever in heaven.

Lord, by Your Cross and resurrection
    You have set us free.
    You are the Savior of the world!

Fish Do the
Strangest Things

First paperback edition, 1990

Text copyright © 1966 by Random House, Inc. Illustrations copyright © 1990 by John F.
Eggert. All rights reserved under International and Pan-American Copyright Conventions.
Published in the United States by Random House, Inc., New York, and simultaneously in
Canada by Random House of Canada Limited, Toronto.

Library of Congress Cataloging-in-Publication Data:
Hornblow, Leonora. Fish do the strangest things / written by Leonora and Arthur Hornblow ;
illustrated by John F. Eggert.   p.   cm.—(Step-up nature books) SUMMARY: Describes seven-
teen fish that have peculiar characteristics and habits, including fish that spit, fly, climb
trees, blow up like balloons, and sleep out of water.   ISBN: 0-394-84309-6 (pbk.);
0-394-94309-0 (lib. bdg.) 1. Fishes—Juvenile literature. [1. Fishes] I. Hornblow,
Arthur.   II. Eggert, John F., ill.   III. Title.   IV. Series.   QL617.2.H66   1989
597– dc19   88-30202

Manufactured in the United States of America   1 2 3 4 5 6 7 8 9 0

Fish Do the Strangest Things

By Leonora and Arthur Hornblow
Illustrated by John F. Eggert

STEP-UP BOOKS

Random House New York

CONTENTS

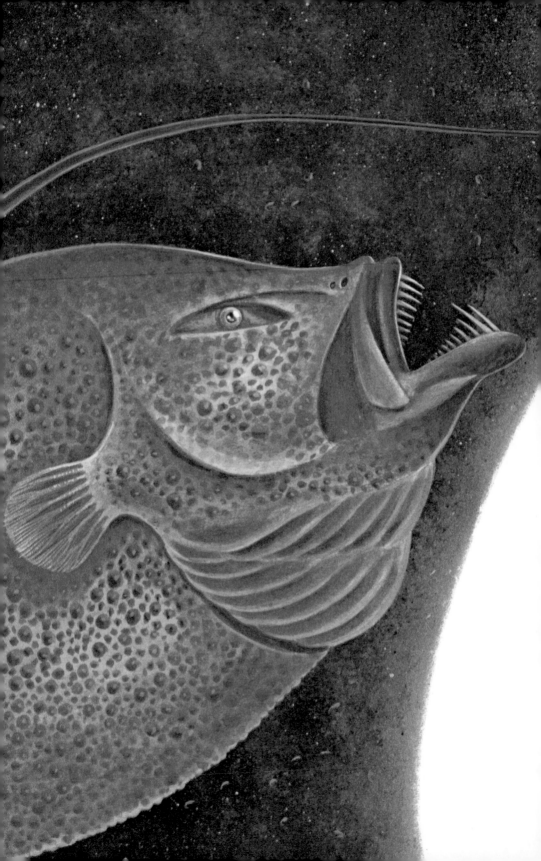

1
THE FISH THAT GOES FISHING

People who fish catch many strange fish. But one of the strangest fish of all does her own fishing. She lives deep down in the dark sea. She is called the deep-sea angler.

The deep-sea angler has her own fishing rod. It grows out of the top of her head and hangs in front of her mouth. The tip of her rod shines in the deep, dark water. This tip is the bait on her fishing rod.

Hungry fish see her bait. They think it

is something to eat. A hungry fish will swim toward the shiny bait. The angler opens her wide mouth. The fish swims closer and closer. He swims right at the bait. Then the angler closes her mouth. Snap! That's the end of that fish.

The female deep-sea angler may grow to be three feet long. But her mate is much smaller. He is only about three inches long.

Almost as soon as he is born, the male angler starts looking for a mate. When he finds one, he fastens onto her side with his mouth. Soon their skin grows together. After this they can never be parted. Now he will never lose her in the dark.

The male angler has no fishing rod. He does not need one. His mate does the fishing for him.

2

THE SHARPSHOOTER

Many fish like to eat insects. One of these is the archer fish. Other fish have to catch insects in their mouths. Not the archer. He can just shoot them down.

The archer points his head at a bug and spits. The drops of water shot from the archer's mouth hit the insect so hard it is knocked out. It falls into the river. The archer swims over and eats it up. He can hit a bug more than three feet away. The little sharpshooter almost never misses.

It is a wonderful way to catch an insect. But don't you try it. Spitting is only for archer fish.

3

LOOK OUT FOR SHARKS

All that you may ever see of a shark at sea is his dark fin cutting through the water. If you want to see more, go to an aquarium. It is safer.

Sharks are very mean-looking fish. Some of them are as mean as they look. Some of them will even eat people.

Even a shark's skin is dangerous. It is covered with tiny sharp scales. The scales are like little teeth. Swimmers have been hurt just brushing against a shark.

The great white shark is a huge fish. In his great mouth there are rows and rows of terrible teeth. He is one of the worst man-eaters.

The hammerhead is just as dangerous as the white shark. And he is much stranger looking. He has one of the oddest heads of

Hammerhead shark

any fish. It is shaped like a hammer. He has one eye at each end of his head. A hammerhead's eyes may be three feet apart.

The biggest fish in the sea is a shark. He is called the whale shark. But this giant fish eats only tiny fish and plants. He does not eat people. A whale shark may even let people ride on him!

Great white shark

Whale shark

It would not be wise to try to ride any other kind of shark. Other sharks cannot be trusted. They may attack at any time. And if there is blood in the water, it drives them crazy. If a fish or a person has been hurt, the sea may suddenly be full of sharks. They attack wildly. If one of the sharks is hurt, the others turn on him. They do not mind eating each other.

But most of the time a shark will look things over before he attacks.

A deep-sea diver may find himself looking right into the face of a big shark. If the diver stays quiet, the shark will probably go away. Most sharks would rather eat fish than people.

There is a silly story that a shark will go away if you hit him on the nose. Sometimes dolphins will do this to fight off a shark. Dolphins are wonderful swimmers. It is all right for them to try it. It is not a good idea for anyone else.

4

THE HITCHHIKER

The remora can travel for thousands of miles beneath the sea without swimming. He has a wonderful way of getting around. He just catches a ride on a bigger fish.

The remora holds on with the top of his head. The top of his head is flat. There is a suction cap on it. With this cap he can quickly fasten onto another fish. He cannot fall off unless he wants to.

The remora rides on sharks so much that he is often called a "shark sucker." Some-

times many remoras will ride at the same time. But remoras will ride on almost any big fish.

The remora gets a free ride. And he also gets free meals. When the big fish catches his dinner, the remora lets go. He swims around and eats up the leftovers. And sometimes he just lets go and goes off fishing for himself.

Some people use the little remora to help them catch big fish or turtles. These fishermen tie a line to the remora's tail. Then they get in their boat. They paddle away from shore. When they see a turtle, they let out their fishing line. Away goes the remora.

The remora quickly fastens onto the turtle. The men in the boat pull the remora in. The turtle is caught just as surely as if it had been hooked. That shows how strong the remora's suction cap is. He is one little fish that really uses his head.

5

THE SLEEPING BEAUTY

Most fish can breathe only underwater. If they are out of water too long, they die. But not the African lungfish. He can live out of water for years. He can breathe air.

The lungfish needs to be able to breathe air. In Africa the hot summer sun may dry up the stream where he lives. Before the stream is all dried up, the lungfish curls up in the mud on the bottom. He leaves a tiny hole in the mud to breathe through. He wraps his tail over his eyes.

The mud gets hard and dry. This does not matter to the lungfish. He is asleep. He will sleep until the rains come. The rains will fill the streams again. They will wash him free of his mud ball.

While a lungfish is in his mud ball he can be dug out of the ground. He can be sent to an aquarium far from his home. At the aquarium the mud ball is opened. This must be done with great care. If the mud ball breaks, so will the lungfish.

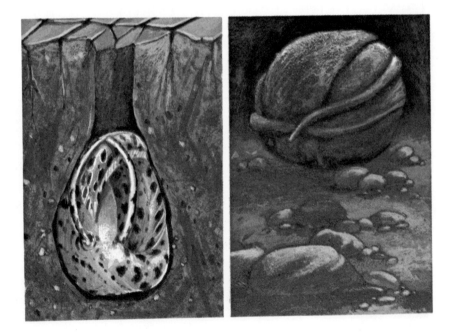

The lungfish has had nothing to eat or drink for a long time. He is much smaller than he was when he went to sleep. He is wrinkled and dry and still curled up.

In a tank of water he straightens out. He eats and eats. Soon he is fatter than ever. He will be all right if he is left alone.

He does not even like another lungfish to share his tank. Sometimes young lungfish will live together for a while without fighting. Then one will bite off the fins and scales of the other. Luckily for lungfish, they can grow new ones. That is one more strange thing about this strange fish from Africa.

6

THE KING OF THE RIVER

Most of the time an alligator gar moves very slowly. He looks like an old log floating in the river. But he is one of the biggest freshwater fish in America. Gars sometimes grow to be 12 feet long.

Gars can live to be very old. It is not easy to kill a gar. A spear will bounce right off him. Indians once used gar skin for armor. And they used gar scales for arrowheads. But a gar has more than his scales to keep him safe. He is a fierce fighter. And he can move quickly if he wants to.

The gar may look something like an alligator. But he can kill an alligator with one bite of his mighty jaws.

For millions of years, alligator gars have been the kings of the southern rivers. But they have never been known to attack a person in the water. So don't worry if that old floating log turns out to be a gar.

24

7
THE FISH WITH WHISKERS

One of the strangest of the river fish is the catfish. Most catfish have eight long feelers on their faces. The feelers make the catfish look as if he has whiskers.

The feelers help a catfish find his food. He can taste with his feelers. He can taste with the rest of his body too. A catfish can even taste with his tail.

The catfish tastes everything he touches. There cannot be many tastes the catfish does not like. Even garbage is fine food for a catfish. This is lucky for us. The catfish helps to keep our rivers clean.

But there is a time when many male catfish do not eat a thing. This is when the eggs are laid by the mother catfish. The father takes the eggs into his mouth. But he does not swallow them.

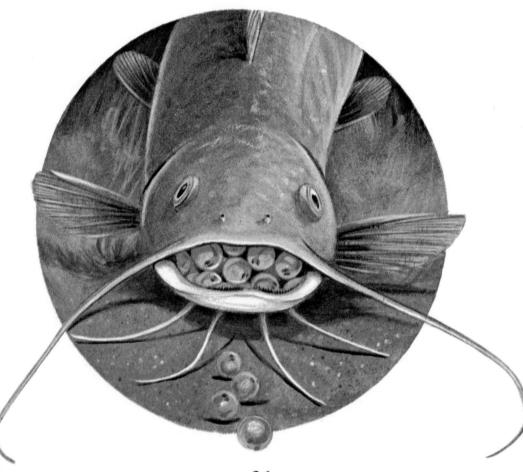

The father catfish keeps the eggs in his mouth until they hatch. Then he just spits the baby catfish out. But he does not leave the little ones. If he sees an enemy, he takes the babies right back into his mouth.

Then one day the father no longer knows his children. He would be glad to eat them himself. Somehow the young catfish know

this. From then on they take care of themselves.

There are more than a thousand kinds of catfish. They are all strange. One of the strangest lives in Africa. He is not at all like the others.

Most catfish stay near the bottom of a river. Not this African catfish. He looks for his food at the top. He rolls over on his back. He swims along upside down. Because of this, he is called the upside-down catfish. Can you think of a better name for him? Even other catfish might find this one strange.

8

THE GREAT JOURNEY

The beautiful king salmon spends almost all his life on a journey. The journey is one of the longest and strangest in the world of fish.

The journey begins in a little pool far from the sea. This is where the salmon are born.

When the baby salmon are a few inches long, they leave their pool. They swim into a stream. The stream grows larger. Other streams join it. The streams become a river.

The river fills with thousands of small salmon. The river is taking them to the sea. It sweeps the salmon over rocks and waterfalls. It sweeps them along tail first! Some of the salmon may have to go two thousand miles to reach the Pacific Ocean. That is a long way to go tail first.

Suddenly the little fish are in the huge ocean. They will live here for about three years. They will swim hundreds and hundreds of miles. They may swim far away from land out into the deep Pacific.

As they swim they eat and eat. They grow bigger and bigger. They grow stronger and stronger. They will need to be strong. The hardest part of their journey is about to begin. Suddenly the salmon stop eating. Somehow they know that it is time to go back to the same little pools they left so long ago.

How can the salmon do this? Salmon have a wonderful sense of smell. They have wonderful memories, too. They remember the smell of the water in the pools where they were born. They now must follow their noses back to their birthplace.

It was easy for the young salmon to come down the rivers to the sea. The rivers just carried them. But now the salmon must go the other way. They must swim against the mighty rivers. They must leap up the waterfalls. They must fight against the waters of the rapids.

JOHN F. EGGERT 1989

The salmon are beaten and bruised by the rocks and the rushing water. They grow weak and tired. But at last most of them reach the pools where they were born. Now there is one more thing they must do. They are just strong enough to do it. The females lay their eggs. The salmon cover the eggs with sand. Then they die. But their work has been done. Soon their eggs will hatch. The river will again be full of young salmon on their way to the sea. Another great journey will begin.

9

THE TIDE RIDERS

Every day the waters of the oceans rise and fall. When the water is low, it is called low tide. When it is high, it is called high tide. Every two weeks there is a very high tide. There are little fish who seem to know all about the tides. They are called grunion.

At night in the spring and summer thousands of grunion swim up onto the California beaches. They swim up on the very high tide. The waves go out. The grunion are left on the beach. Right away the female grunion start digging. They dig with their tails.

Soon they are half buried in the soft, wet sand. Then they lay their eggs. They must do this before the next wave comes in. When the next wave comes in, the grunion wiggle down to it. It takes them back to the sea.

The eggs stay in the sand for two weeks. Then the next very high tide washes over them. Out pop the baby grunion. The waves carry them out to sea. They will stay in the sea for a year. Then they will ride the tide back to the beaches to lay their own eggs.

10

THE GREAT MYSTERY

Eels are strange creatures. They look like snakes. They move like snakes. But they are fish.

For thousands of years, eels had a secret. How were young eels born? Where were they born? Nobody knew. Nobody had ever seen an eel egg. Nobody had ever seen a baby eel. The secret of the eels was found out far from their freshwater homes.

Out in the Atlantic Ocean people had seen fish that looked like tiny glass leaves. Two men caught a few of these fish and kept them in a tank of water. The men got a big surprise. The tiny fish turned into little eels.

Now people knew that eels came from the sea. But how did they get there? A man named Johannes Schmidt wanted to find out. He asked ships' captains to help him. The captains watched for the tiny glass fish. They caught many for Dr. Schmidt. For 17 years he studied them. At last he knew the secret of the eels.

Female eels live most of their lives far from the sea. They live in ponds and rivers and streams. Some even live in wells. Then the time comes for them to lay their eggs. They swim down the rivers to the ocean. There the male eels are waiting for them. Together they swim out into the ocean. They swim and swim. At last they come to a place called the Sargasso Sea. All the eels from Europe and America come there. And

there, deep in the sea, they lay their eggs.
Then they die.

After a week the eggs hatch. The baby
eels now look like glass leaves. They look
just like the ones Dr. Schmidt studied. The

baby American eels float and swim toward America. The baby European eels move toward Europe. No one knows how this can be. That is one secret the eels still keep to themselves.

Before they reach the rivers, the little glass fish change into little eels. The females leave the males. The females find homes far from the ocean. Years go by. They grow strong and fat. Then one day they start back down the rivers. They meet the waiting male eels. Together they will make the long, long journey back to the Sargasso Sea.

11

THE BALLOON

The puffer fish is small. He is a slow swimmer. But he has a wonderful way of keeping himself safe. When he sees a big fish coming, he does not swim away. He just puffs himself up.

He does this by swallowing air or water. This makes him look like a balloon.

The big fish may be scared away by this sudden change. If the big fish is not scared away, he will find that the round puffer is quite a mouthful.

The strangest puffer of all is called the porcupine fish. His skin is covered with sharp scales. When he puffs himself up, his scales stick out all over. Any fish that swallowed him would have a very sore throat.

Sometimes puffers do a silly thing. They keep on puffing up and puffing up until— *pop* goes the puffer.

12

OLD BIG NOSE

The swordfish has the longest and sharpest "nose" in the world of fish. It is really part of his jaw. It has two very sharp edges. It is shaped like a big flat sword. And the swordfish uses it like a sword.

Into a school of fish the mighty swordfish swims. He slashes his sword all around. Soon he has cut up a fine meal for himself.

The swordfish likes to eat fish. And many people like to eat swordfish. But swordfish are not easy to catch. Nets cannot hold them. They slash their way out with their swords.

Today people have learned how to catch swordfish with hooks. This is much safer for people than it used to be. Swordfish used to be speared with harpoons. Often the swordfish would fight back. He might even attack the boat. The swordfish is so fast and so strong that he can run his sword right into a wooden boat.

Sometimes sailors on the boat were badly hurt. Sometimes the boat would even sink to the bottom of the sea.

The swordfish's sword is a mighty weapon. But he is not born with it. The baby swordfish has teeth. As he grows, so does his sword. He loses his teeth. He does not need teeth with that sword.

13

THE FISH WITH WINGS

The flying fish looks like a little model airplane. But the flying fish does not fly. He glides.

The flying fish swims to the top of the water as fast as he can. He skims along for a bit. Then he flips his tail and up he goes.

We think the flying fish leaves the water to get away from his enemies. He can stay in the air for almost a minute. Then down he comes with a splash. Often he will just flip his tail and take off again.

The winds may carry him high above the water. Sometimes at night flying fish will glide right onto the deck of a boat. They may have gotten away from a hungry dolphin. But now they will be a wonderful breakfast for a hungry sailor.

14

THE FLYING SAUCERS

Rays are strange-looking fish. Some of them are very small. Some of them are very big. Most of them are very, very flat.

The round stingray is a small ray. He is as round and flat as a plate. He lives along the seashore. He likes muddy water. He is the color of mud. It is hard to see him lying flat in the mud.

It is not hard for the stingray to see you. His eyes are on top of his head. This helps him to watch out for enemies.

The stingray has a strange way of fighting his enemies. He fights with his tail. On his tail he has a stinger. There is poison on the stinger. It is a terrible weapon.

People may step on round stingrays by mistake. People who do can be badly hurt. If you think there are stingrays around, drag your feet. The rays will get out of your way. Like everyone else, the stingray does not like to be stepped on.

The little round stingray does not go out into the deep sea. But there are many rays that do. The sea is the home of the biggest ray of all. He is the manta ray. He is called "the giant devilfish." That sounds fierce. But he is not. He has no stinger. And he eats only very small fish. He sweeps them into his mouth as he swims.

It is wonderful to watch a manta swimming. His sides flap up and down like huge wings. He looks like a big black bat flying underwater.

An even stranger thing to see is a manta leaping. He jumps high in the air. When the giant manta comes down, he comes down with a giant crash. Sometimes two or three mantas will all leap at once. The great crash of their landing sounds like thunder across the sea.

15

THE HANGER-ON

In the sea there is a tiny fish that does not look at all like a fish. He is called the sea horse. When you see him, you know why. His head is like the head of a tiny, tiny horse. But the rest of him is not shaped like a horse. It is not shaped like a fish, either. It is just strange.

One very strange thing about the sea horse is his tail. He can hang on to things with it the way a monkey can.

Most of the time the sea horse just hangs

on to plants underwater. When he wants to go to another plant, he lets go and swims away.

He does not swim the way other fish do. It looks as if he is standing on his tail. And he swims very slowly. There is only one part of the sea horse that moves fast. It is the tiny fin on his back. Back and forth it goes. It pushes the sea horse through the water to another plant.

It is lucky that the slow sea horse does not have to chase his food. He just sucks in bits of food that float by. He has no teeth.

The slow, toothless little sea horse cannot fight off enemies. But bigger fish have trouble seeing him. He hides in the seaweed and other plants. Some sea horses can even change their color. They can change to the color of the plants.

The strangest thing about sea horses is the way their babies are born. The mother

sea horse lays about 200 eggs. She lays them in a little pocket on the father's stomach. He carries them around until they hatch. Then the baby sea horses wiggle and twist in the father's pocket. To help them get out, the father wiggles and twists too.

The babies pop out into the sea. Right away the baby sea horses start grabbing at things with their tails. They have not learned what to hold on to. They may even try to hold on to air bubbles. They soon learn. They find a plant. They hang on to it and watch the underwater world go by.

16

THE TREE CLIMBER

You never know where you may find a fish. But what a surprise it would be to find a fish in a tree. It happens. There really is a fish that can climb a tree! His name is the mudskipper.

The mudskipper climbs trees to catch insects. He pulls himself up the tree with his front fins. They are almost like little legs. He cannot climb very high. But it is amazing that a fish can climb a tree at all.

The mudskipper spends some time in the

water. But he is out of the water as much as he is in it.

He walks and skips and jumps around on the mud flats. When he wants to skip quickly, he pushes himself along with his tail. He can skip faster than a person can follow him. It is a funny sight to see a mudskipper skip.

The mudskipper does so many things that are strange for a fish to do. Do you suppose the mudskipper knows that he is a fish?

17

THE LITTLE DOCTOR

Most little fish get out of the way when they see a big fish coming. Most little fish are afraid the big fish will eat them. Most of the time the little fish are right.

But there is one little fish that goes right up to the big fish. He puts his head in the big fish's mouth. He even swims between the teeth of the terrible moray eel. This strange little fish is called the wrasse.

His name really should be the "little doctor fish." The little doctor cleans the teeth of the bigger fish. He cleans their eyes. He cleans their fins. He takes away little things that are growing on the other fish. These things would make the fish sick if the little doctor did not clean them off. That is why the wrasse is not bitten by the big fish. They seem to know that he is helping them. They even wait their turn to see him. They are like people waiting in a real doctor's office.

It is wonderful to think that fish have their own doctors. But this is only one of the wonders of the fish world.

Scientists have always wanted to know more about the world of fish. It is a big world. There is more water in the world than there is land.

Scientists now think we, too, will be able to live underwater some day. If this ever happens, who can tell what strange new things we will find out about our neighbors, the fish?